BECOMING
WHAT
YOU ARE

Also by Two Workers

The Seven Laws of Spiritual Purity

BECOMING WHAT YOU ARE

A CONCISE GUIDE TO AWAKENING THE LIGHT WITHIN

TWO WORKERS

Radiant Books

New York

Becoming What You Are was originally published as *Awaken! Children of the Light!* in 1918. Illustrations by Romain Bonnet.

Library of Congress Control Number: 2023939498

Published in 2023 by Radiant Books
radiantbooks.co

ISBN 978-1-63994-039-4 (hardback)
ISBN 978-1-63994-040-0 (paperback)
ISBN 978-1-63994-041-7 (e-book)

CONTENTS

III. Ever Onward!

PREFACE

THE WORDS in this booklet were addressed to us by a Higher Consciousness. Whether this was a Master, the Inner Self, or another Helper of Humanity — this is left to every reader's intuition to find out.

Being an imperative call for the active demonstration of all that ennobles and uplifts, we supposed that much of what was given to us might help others.

Hence, we selected from our teachings the more impersonal ones and arranged them into the chapters of this book.

The quick exhaustion of the first edition, the scores of appreciative letters received by the publishers, the early requests for foreign editions — these have proven that it is answering the purpose with which it was sent out: to "awaken" many.

May it evermore be read, and its precepts be scrupulously applied by all under whose eyes it comes.

The Writers
Krotona, July 1918

I

THE CALL

Wake up, all you
who are in pain
and sorrow — and
listen to His call!

Awaken!

Awaken, O children of the New Humanity, and see and realize your glorious destiny.

Wake up from your dullness and indifference — and use your powers.

Fill your hearts with love for one another and live a life of oneness and unity.

Realize your possibilities now — and follow the Voice of Our Great Helper.

We need all who can respond to His call.

All who belong to Him must wake up from their useless dreams of good-for-nothing, petty, selfish desires.

Everyone must realize their place in the work of helping all that are in darkness and ignorance. Help to lift their consciousness to the realization of the power of good and make them see the great responsibility of this Divine message.

We, the Masters of the Wisdom, are pleading to be heard.

We need you — We need all.

O, that all would wake up and help Him, the Great Lord of the World — and help Us in the tremendous work for which the whole of humankind is waiting!

The note is sounded.

How many will respond?

"I Am"

I am your Master.

And I am more than that; for I am you yourself — and you are I Myself.

I am you — you are I — We are He — all are One.

I am where you are.

I am the Light of your soul. Always call Me so — and become that Light to others.

I am the spirit within your heart — and everywhere I am, in everybody's heart.

Right in the heart of all that lives am I.

I am in all — and am all.

Think about this till you can never again mistake anyone as separate from Me — for I am they — and everyone is I.

I look through everybody's eyes — you want to see Me there always.

Think of Me as the Power which is helping and guiding.

I am in all help, in all sacrifice — and in helping others, you make yourself one with Me.

I am Love — and every expression of pure love is an expression of Myself.

Listen to My Voice — and never miss an opportunity to bring My words among people.

The Great Helpers

We are the Good in the world.

We flood the world with light — but people are incarcerated in a shell of selfish interests through which no light can break.

Our duties are far above your conception — and Our work is quite different from that of Our pupils.

They are the instruments through which We can help and work.

Help to bring Us out in yourself — and, if you can, in others.

Through others is the way to Us.

We will help you — and you know that, then, everything is possible.

We shall help all as they need it: everyone in their own way.

We can only help you when you open up yourself for Our forces.

It is only for the help of others that Our force can be used.

Live to help and to sustain, to protect and to strengthen — and Our forces will stream through you as life-giving power.

See Our aim as that of helping humanity to realize its possibilities.

Every day is your opportunity to come nearer to Us.

We are there, and We are ready for you — but you must come to Us and do the climbing yourself.

The Lord of Love

It is He, the great One, to whom you belong as love belongs to love — which is itself.

It is He, whom you must see in all: all is He — He is all.

He is your Savior and Brother, who gives His life every second to bring you nearer to your Self.

Love is His Breath of Life, with which He helps the human hearts to unfold their Divine powers.

All love is He — is His manifestation.

Love is the only way to reach Him — the One who is Love incarnate.

All can reach Him — if their will is strong enough.

Believe in His power, His mighty help — and let His Light shine into your soul and radiate into the world through your acts and words.

Always think about what He wants you to do.

Nothing unworthy of Him may ever come or pass through you.

Love Him with your whole being — and raise your consciousness to His love for you. Pour forth His love with the same strength as you get it.

In loving others, you love Him.

Be sure to follow His idea of love: He loves every atom, every living creature, every human being — no matter what they are or do.

Love them in His way.

Every breath of you must send His love to the world.

The Christ Within

He is the One who rules the heart of everyone — whoever it may be.

From the heart, all actions can be ruled by Him, the Love of all the world.

Find Him within yourself. Think of Him more as always being in your Heart.

Think of Him as being in you and all the others, too. Yes, as the Great Being manifesting in all that lives and is.

Awaken Him within you to always fuller expression — and suppress all that is not He.

Help to awaken Him in others.

As He can find expression in their hearts, all will be benefited from His Presence.

His first touch is the conception of the Christ child. It will grow within, become stronger always and make you purer and better.

But it develops by pain — never forget this.

Every pain will strengthen it — and then it will soon be born and make you one of Us.

The Coming Teacher

The Great Lord of Love is coming soon — and much has to be done before He can begin His task in the lower phases of expression.

His Coming is the most glorious event for ages to come.

In His Hands rests the equilibrium of the world; He keeps the scales of good and evil balanced.

He is approaching ever more and more — and as He comes nearer, stronger grows the resistance of those whose task is to oppose evolution and test humanity's strength.

That in itself is proof of His approach.

He must be heard over the whole world. His Voice must be understood, even before He comes.

Try to make the people realize the nearness of Him, whom the world needs and cries for in despair.

It does cry for Him.

He will come sooner than anyone now thinks: He is counting the hours that separate Him from the outer world.

His influence is already over the Earth.

Receive Him even now — by living His love, His beauty, His purity.

Why He Comes

To bring love and harmony and the Light of Divine Oneness to humanity is His work.

No sacrifice is too great for your Divine Brother.

All will depend on the stage humanity can reach with this effort of the Helping Hands stretched out in merciful pity.

He is waiting to fight the battle for the victory of love supreme.

Humanity now has the choice of light or misery.

Soon it will have crossed its darkest age — and light will shine where darkness reigned.

Eternal joy and expansion await their expression — and sorrow and pain will soon belong to a shadowy past.

Glory and happiness are awaiting humanity — theirs to grasp.

With one great effort, their suffering can now cease.

If they will see His Light, turn to it, and realize His Love — then will it cease.

Peace will reign on Earth in the age that He comes to bring to you.

Peace, based on love — Peace, breaking down the barriers between race and race, between nation and nation, between classes and castes.

Truth Divine will enlighten the world when He comes.

But humanity must wake up — and be worthy of His and Our help.

Much must be changed and many helped before He can be among you.

Listen to His call, all who are in the fetters of selfishness and ignorance.

See your duty and possibilities in the work He wants you to do for Him.

Preparing His Way

Help the work of preparation for the Coming of the Lord of Love — by living love and giving His love to all.

Speak about Him to all.

Do not miss a single opportunity to spread the tidings — so that many may respond when the time is ripe.

Make the world see Him as He manifests Himself in the spreading of fraternity among humankind, for which so many movements now are working.

Tell them they will see Him only if they are looking in the direction where He stands: on the path of kinship and love.

The world must be brought closer and closer into touch with His teachings: make them familiar to all.

Make people realize the enormous effort made now in the starting of the New Humanity.

Make them understand the importance of this turning point, where the Light is offered once more.

To help others to reach Him — this must be your only aim.

Much can be done now, and a better result will be gained by all that is done now than by all that can be done when He comes.

Use all your energy to make His influence stronger.

Prepare His Way in every possible way.

Follow Him!

The Lord of Love, when He comes, will need many channels to do His work with Him: to bring His Message of Love and Compassion to humanity.

Many are needed — and few are ready.

I now come to call together all the workers who are willing to be trained for Him.

I come to many these days to make them ready for the work that is to be done soon.

These are strenuous times for all who can see the importance of the new cycle — and Our disciples must increase in number and strength to carry the work through.

We need all the workers We can get and train for certain work — each in their own strongest side, and always for the same purpose.

When He comes, the world must be prepared to recognize Him — and much will depend on how Our disciples obey Our hints.

Theirs is the karma of their readiness to help in this great work — and they cannot overestimate the call of the hour.

It is a great responsibility that rests upon Our pupils — but love for Him will enable them to always work more effectively for and with Him.

They must be Our outposts in the world — and their aim must be, constantly, this: how to do Our work to make a better humanity.

All that will spread His teachings, His doctrine of love and sacrifice, is Our work and their work.

Stand together — and be convinced of My help.

Receive Him within yourself — and be His worker now that He needs you.

Tell others about the need for vehicles for Our forces — and in the meantime: let all know that the Great Lord is ready to come.

We protect and love you ever more for all you are willing to bear for Him, the Master of all Masters.

II

HOW TO
QUALIFY

Go on and grow —
and be a helper
soon, instead of one
who only needs
much help.

Discrimination

We cannot use puppets and people who have no discrimination!

We want workers who can do independent work.

We want cooperation — and for that, you must develop the knowledge of what matters and what does not.

We will test your common sense very often — for you must learn to stand alone so that We can trust you.

What We want of you is to depend upon your own strong mind.

You must learn that only you must decide whatever the personality must do or not and in what way.

Know that We never force things upon Our disciples.

Seriously know that you are right to the best of your self-knowledge — and then do that — even if it is against Our express wishes.

Even your faith in Us may not interfere with your own inherent power.

The independent way of thinking and acting must be developed so strongly that you will always be sure to carefully discriminate before you say, do, or even think.

Live discrimination in all things: extremes are never wise.

Scrutinize whatever I have said — for you know I want those who think for themselves.

No Blind Obedience

We need independent, thinking helpers, who can judge for themselves, and never blindly obey.

Always think of Us and what We would do — then you will know also. But never blindly obey without understanding.

Better use your own judgment, and make a mistake — than blindly obey Us, even.

Only by making yourself a strong and self-willed instrument, a pure and strong channel for Our force, can you do the work of helping all whom you possibly can reach.

Better a wrong deed, provided you have carefully considered it all — than the right deed against your own conviction.

Where you obeyed Me blindly, you obeyed neither your will nor Mine.

Faith

Absolute faith is necessary.

Faith is different from blind obedience.

Faith is knowledge — and you must always grow in wisdom and understanding of the Divine Law, which is the Law you must follow.

If you follow Our Laws, I am always with you.

Realize My presence — and grow a stronger faith in Me.

I stand behind you in all unselfish work to help your fellow neighbors.

Whenever you call Me, I come and pour My love and strength into you. And then you can go on and on and not get worn out.

The source of strength is in your faith in Me.

Faith is strength.

Your trust in Us is not the main thing to be learned: what you must also learn is to trust in your own Self.

You must trust yourself and Us and not go by the opinions and thoughts of others, no matter what they are. They may be very good for them, but you must trust your inner God — and know Us as such.

Trust your own powers and become more positive.

Do not weaken your power by doubt.

Trust your intuition — which will never fail you when you reach out to it.

Failing to trust yourself is failing Me.

Love one another and trust your fellow workers — or nothing can be achieved.

Love and trust all.

Love: Its Power

Love is the potent power in the Universe by which all exist.

Love is the rhythm in every atom; love is the beat in every heart. Love is the cry of the soul.

Love is all-powerful.

Love more, and you will soon have the power created by love.

Use its force, and the strength of the Universe will be understood.

Love is the Divine in all — whenever you live in love, the Divine manifests in you and can touch others through you.

There is no higher Law than Love.

Love is the power that rules the world; all that is done for its sake has the power of Universal Law behind it.

Do not mistake sentimentality for love — love is the willingness to help.

Only love can conquer evil.

Love is the magic word for liberty, power, and realization.

Nothing but love will overcome the obstacles on your path.

Without the power of love, creation could not be — and you have to wake up and realize that love is the only power that can redeem the world and set the soul free.

If there were no love, how could the world go on?

Through love, it came into existence — through love, it will be redeemed.

But you must do it — We can only help and show it the way.

Love: The Only Way

Love is the only thing that will show you how to reach Us.

Never think for one moment that other qualities are of the same importance; if you had them all and not love, you could never become One with Our work, which is done by love only.

And if you have enough love, all the rest will come in time.

Love everybody and everything, and you will always come nearer to Us.

Make yourself ready and worthy: your greater love will show your growth. It must become universal.

It is not enough to have love: you must give love — live love — *become* love — till you are one with Us in everything.

Meditate on love as the one quality by which you can help Him — and will bring you into Our Brotherhood.

You are the Path if you live love.

Love in Action

Make love a reality around you, not a vague thing far away from you.

It is there: use it, live it, give it to all, without exceptions.

You must love all — never mind whether they deserve it according to your idea.

Every soul is dear to Us, and you must love them all as Our vehicle.

Give love abundantly, always — no matter what others do to you.

Be pure and strong — and love! Yes: know and love.

Live love evermore — till it becomes the beat of your heart, the very breath of your life.

You must manifest love as your own life — which it is.

But *you* must do it: We cannot love the world for you.

Bring love wherever you go.

Love, always more love, must and can be lived by Our disciples — till, at last, they are a living expression of love and helpfulness.

Become so filled with love that no thought which does not carry its message ever leaves your consciousness.

Let love flow through you as naturally as the perfume leaves the flower — and let all near you inhale that Divine breath.

Heal the world with love.

Live it first — and teach it to all.

Kindness

A kindness done to others is a kindness done to Us.

When you injure others — if only by thought or mentioning their failings — you hurt Us, your Masters.

For We are all One — great and small.

Be kind to all without distinction.

All are your kin and My children.

Fight against all that separates you from others — then you can be a helper in My work.

I never want anything to be done which can hurt anyone in the least.

Even if it may seem to be better and wiser, whatever can hurt a person may not be done by My disciples.

Never speak unkindly.

Do not allow unkind thoughts to enter your mind.

Poison is such talk — and all such thoughts are detrimental.

Never again may an unkind thought weaken your power, your progress toward the Great Brotherhood.

Shut the door of your mind when they knock to enter. Never allow them to come in.

Replace them with kind, helpful thoughts.

Practice that faithfully — and they will soon knock in vain and not return anymore.

Always give love — and always be kind, gentle, and humble.

Yet, where it concerns the work, the helping of humanity, you must be able to express your and Our power to its fullest extent.

We need strong helpers.

The Lower Kingdoms

Feel yourself in every atom around you — in humans and beasts, in element and rhythm.

Love all alike.

Follow the Voice of Love — and never for one-second rule your conduct by other motives.

Love is always purer and stronger — so reaching the One Heart in all.

In the Great Heart, there is no difference.

All are fed by one lifeblood.

All are so closely connected that they are affecting each other constantly.

As long as you see difference, there is an absence of love — because love is the life in all.

Live it — and give it to all creatures, without exception.

Love all life. All are expressions of His life, His love.

Work for both animals and people.

Teach the people love for the helpless little things.

Compassion for all is what We want Our disciples to express; it counts more than anything in this world.

All is One — and animals are just as near to Him as the more highly evolved beings.

The Universal Heart beats in the minutest life — and the Great All-Father feels and breathes in all life.

Ponder over that One Great Being, whose expression is everything — and feel your close relationship to all living creatures.

Help the animals, help the plants, with more love and patience — and so, you will hasten the Coming of the Light, which He will bring and establish on Earth forever.

Unify your true Self with the Self of all, and feel your Oneness with all life.

All life is alike — only the form limits its expression.

Oneness

Make your consciousness one with all life around you — and see Me in all.

All are but particles of Myself, and Nature, too, is such and all that is.

Always think of Me and you as One; and also of Him, and even of the Highest you can but think of, as One with all — with the least developed, as well as with the highest imaginable.

We are all One: the One Divine Flame.

Unity and love must become actual reality and not mere words.

Without love, unity never can be realized — because love is oneness with all. Unselfish love is the All-life.

If you are love, you cannot help enveloping the whole world in it — because then, and not before then, you will realize that the world is yourself.

Yes, you know it mentally, but that is not enough.

You are others.

You are all rays of the same Light, of the same Life — and you must feel that unity.

You are part of the One in whom you live and breathe: only a little spark in that Great Being in whom you feel as One with all.

Now realize your Oneness with all the other manifested parts.

Do not anymore allow yourself to think in terms of separateness.

Live in the All instead of in the small, separated part — and you will experience the fullness of the All-embracing Life.

Think of unity — and place your consciousness outside the form, becoming one with the All-consciousness.

Will to see the unity of all manifestation, and soon you *will* know that your life is in all alike.

Realize unity — live in unity with all that come near you.

All people are One.

Help that One evolve toward a fuller expression on the lower planes of Its Divinity.

The perfection of one unit helps the Whole.

From self to Self

Learn the joy of the Great Self by forgetting your own interests, your own longings, and your own desires.

Give up self with all its pettiness and live in the Great Self that manifests all around you.

Think of your Higher Self as being the Self of others.

The Great Self is others, always.

Come out of the darkness of the small self into the light of the All — the one real Existence which includes all life.

Never forget that you are the All: what you give to others, you give to your real Self.

You are not yet enough your Self to always know on the physical plane what it is best to do.

Be your real Self always — and allow no other influences to draw you aside.

Let not the subtlety of the personality ensnare you.

Forget self to reach the Great Heart, which sobs in every human heart.

Realize more and more your true nature — and renounce the smaller for the greater, the fleeting for the real source of all expression.

All that you want for yourself brings pain and disappointment.

Kill out the principle of wishing things for yourself — and above the seeming emptiness is the glory of all-embracing life.

Give yourself to the Great One who will soon come among you; serve Him instead of your little self.

No one can be His helper without love and willingness to sacrifice the lower to the Higher.

Work for and with Him till your whole self becomes Himself. Only by becoming more like Him can He be understood.

He is your true Self.

Use all your strength in fighting against the tempting power of self-gratification and ignorance.

By forgetting yourself and always thinking of Us, you can draw Our strength, Our power into yourself — but only by forgetting yourself.

All that belongs to the personality must lose its importance.

It is the greatest help that you can bring to it, the feeling that it must obey you — and that it has nothing to say.

Let it be My servant to do the outer work: to take care of the physical arrangement which must serve to make My work possible in the best possible way.

See the urgency for help in this critical period of the world's evolution — and be Our instrument to push the Wheel of Life toward an understanding of the purpose of Creation.

Be able to stand aside in all you do.

Your personality must work and think and speak under the controlling power of your real Self, your true "I."

No mistakes are possible once that Self is understood.

Service

Service is the watchword along the road to Me: service cheerfully rendered and with love for all.

You must only have one thought: how to serve best every minute of the day.

Be willing to be the least among the servers.

Be humble as the least among humanity.

Measure your stage with Ours.

Only by doing the little acts of service perfectly well can you prepare for the greater work.

As long as the little things are brought on your path, it is those that We want you to attend to.

Every day you must grow in love and devotion for the coming Teacher and His work.

Let all other things go. Make your life one dedication to Him — and live only for Him, the Blessed One, without whom the burden of the world would be unbearable.

All good, unselfish work is His work — and in helping others, you make yourself one with Him.

Never think for one moment that you can serve Him in better ways than by helping all who come on your path.

Help everyone who comes to you for help — but be careful not to try to interfere with other people's business.

As long as you do not know, it is better to help, even where it proves to be useless — than to miss one opportunity where help is expected from you.

Be ready to help — always.

Give!

Love and give. Give always. Many need your help.

Give what you have to all.

Every minute of your life must be given to Him — to the world.

All your acts must now be done with the thought of giving of all you are, of all you have, to forward the great work for human growth.

Give where it is needed — not for your own pleasure.

Gladly give to others what you most desire for yourself.

Be willing to yield everything, every progress, for the sake of helping others.

Make your whole life one act of unselfish giving of yourself — and We will soon be able to help you to reach the Path.

By giving, you can never lose.

Ask Nothing

The sun sends out its light for others — giving without asking. That is your example.

Radiate love and light from the center within your heart; let love go out to all — but do not draw it toward yourself.

Send it out without the longing that it may return to warm you.

Work for the sake of the work, not the pleasure it gives you.

Love for what you can give, not for what it can give you.

Forget yourself in asking nothing for yourself — and all will be yours in a consciousness, wider and fuller than you can now realize.

Not Even Recognition

Give up self — ask nothing; no recognition for what you do.

All recognition strengthens the personality, whether you recognize it or not.

Purify the lower self by renouncing the world's love and approbation — and do not forget that your nearest surroundings are your world: your bitterest lessons will come from there.

Expect nothing from the world: your approval must come from within.

If there is love, real love, then recognition has no purpose.

It sometimes fills the place when love is absent.

So, do not want it.

The thought that you work for the mighty Source of all love — and for Us, the expression of love — must be enough.

Ask nothing else.

We are your judges — and We look for quite other things than people.

Serenity

Be still when you want to listen to My Voice.

To hear it, you must always be serene and poised.

Perfect quiet of all the bodies is needed when you want to be serene.

Be calm and restful, and compose the bodies constantly. You can do that by thinking of Me.

Turn your thoughts consciously to Us.

We know no impatience — and you must try to become as We are.

Do that regularly, and will to be calm and poised — then We can use your bodies better.

Our disciples must be balanced and firm as a rock: indifferent to their own troubles yet sensitive and responsive to the difficulties and sorrows of others.

Nothing may disturb your equilibrium — nothing, whether praise, blame, failure, or success.

Be balanced in pleasure and pain, joy and grief, with unshaken patience and ever-growing faith in your Divine Self.

Everything you do must be done consciously: never be spontaneous or impulsive.

No matter what happens to you, be strong and unruffled, and use Our power — the power of understanding.

Never allow yourself to get excited or nervous — because then, We can help you, but very little.

Be calm — and His strength will help you.

Harmony

You are anxious to help all to be harmonious. You can more and more do by being so yourself.

Purify your surroundings with vibrations of peace and harmony — and then others will do the same.

Do not add new discord to the scale, which already is difficult enough to keep in balance — the scale of wrong and right.

Bring out the true spirit of kinship in your own life.

Realize the power of harmonious cooperation; strive to live it with everybody everywhere.

Love and harmony are necessary requirements, and it is only by their power that a group can work as a channel for Our work.

That glorious time shall come; when all who work for Him will stand together before the world and work as one — united by devotion and love for Him and all that lives.

Real sympathy is expressed by placing your consciousness in others — and with your experience thinking in them.

Think as they think — and, in your consciousness, see and find the solution for their difficulties.

Only by linking your consciousness to that of others can sympathy be given.

Help where you can to harmonize each one.

Peace

A lasting peace will be the outcome of this war. I shall use its suffering to teach My Love to the world— for only in this way can love and kinship be developed. And as the suffering grows, so will the result be greater.

Universal Peace must be reached soon; every channel by which it can be accomplished is necessary — and is helped by Us.

There is little time left — and the tide must turn through humanity's efforts.

Work hard for peace.

Every worker has to do tenfold work in these days of tension — and the power they can use is great.

Think of peace over the Earth — every hour, every minute.

This is important to prepare His way and make His Coming among humanity possible.

Feel the Peace eternal. Vibrate calmness. Send out peace and serenity.

Every empty minute you must fill with this thought.

Put more strength into your meditation on Peace.

Put more will into your thought.

That is what is needed now — so do it.

Justice

Mercy is your part — justice, Ours!

Forget justice for mercy, righteousness for love.

This counts for all — not only friends and people you like.

Mercy, love, and kindness belong to a higher plane than justice.

Only when intuition and mind have become one expression of Divine power can you understand justice as We do.

The fact that you have outgrown the law of Moses: "an eye for an eye, and a tooth for a tooth" — and that you now must follow the Lord of Mercy and Compassion — this is not yet clearly understood.

The soul must first learn justice and then be willing to sacrifice justice for love's sake — before it can express Divine Justice, which is the same as love.

Divine Law is Love — Divine Justice is Love. They are One.

Always love first. Leave justice to Us.

Forgiveness

All that others do to you — little unkind acts, injustices, thoughtless words — belongs to the unreal. It only affects the personality, the lower self, which is unreal and ephemeral.

All that you grow in love and forgiveness and kindness belongs to the real — because it makes you reach out to the Higher Self, which is real.

Try to feel love for the one who injures you by raising your consciousness to their Higher Self — which is your Self.

Forgiveness exists no more when you really love.

Always forgive; return hatred by love, unkindness by gentleness — and help your enemies mentally.

Help them as you desire to be helped by Us.

As long as you are unwilling to lay down your life for an enemy's sake, you have not yet realized unity — and your way of helping is still influenced by your personality.

Do for others what you would love to have done for yourself.

Think of others with the same forgiveness which each soul has for itself.

Give — and forgive, My Children.

Criticism

We are the Ones to judge — not you.

For We see everything, and you can only see very little.

Other people's shortcomings are not your business.

You have to correct your own failings — and that is what each person must do, sometimes.

Each comes to Us along their own road — and no one but We know where they stand.

Can you not see that all are only unfolding and in the process of growth?

Practice this way of judging others, and soon you will not be able to judge at all, but you will see the unfolding beauty of Divine power everywhere and in all.

Mistakes will very likely be made — by you as well as others.

But every mistake will bring its lesson.

If you do not make them anymore, you are perfect — and that is not yet to be expected of any one of you.

Think of this before critical thoughts take shape.

You must close your mind before such a thought can enter and impress itself on your brain.

It must be done artificially, as long as you still see imperfection as detestable.

Take yourself in hand earnestly — and soon, you will only see the good in others and the ego's efforts to develop its vehicle.

Let nothing seduce you to judge, no matter whomsoever it may be.

You only injure yourself and your own progress — without improving conditions or helping people to become better.

Thoughts

No thought — no word — is hidden from Us.

I am always watching all your thoughts; they are reflected in My consciousness.

Watch every thought, lest your progress is not as rapid as it could be.

Your mind is still full of old thought waves to which you may not give new strength.

You must now make new vibrations in your mind and practice them daily.

That is what your meditation is for.

Your life and meditation must become one — and every thought must be so pure that it might belong to your meditation.

Always have your mind pure and receptive to Our help.

Every thought which is not absolutely pure and unselfish shuts you off from Us.

Watch your thoughts: they are the sources of all that will result in acts.

Think purity, and your acts will be pure and beneficial.

Restrain evil thoughts; they must die out and never be given new strength.

Only old thinking habits are between you and the light of perfect love. Your task is to replace them by loving helping thoughts till such thoughts become a habit.

Use your mind for the upliftment of the world all the time.

Fill it only with beautiful thoughts — and, by doing so, diminish the unhappiness on Earth.

Your thoughts are your children — and you must make every one of them beautiful and useful for Us.

Make your thoughts strong and definite, and send them out as an army of helpful forces for Us.

Every thought must have the power to bring balance where the Law is broken — to restore equilibrium where others failed.

Every thought must be constructive, helping the forces for good.

His disciples must make His work easier — and every impure thought makes it harder.

Your thoughts about others must always have His power within them.

Unworthy thoughts could not be strengthened by Him. He would purify them with His purity — but so, you increase His work instead of lightening the burden He has to bear.

Your thoughts must be so filled with love that they become healing streams to help the world.

Useless Thoughts

Every useless thought is wasted energy.

You should not waste a single thought.

Learn to conserve your forces: do not waste even the smallest part of your energy on useless thoughts or things.

Let every thought work for Us.

Exclude from your mind all that is unnecessary and useless, and you will have more strength for what is helpful and necessary.

Only helpful vibrations must leave your brain.

Make it a habit to shut out all useless thoughts — and no longer let any such thoughts form into words and phrases.

It is not enough that your thoughts are not bad. They must become helpful and in the direction of active good.

Every thought must have a purpose and be sent out with definite work to do.

Whenever you think useless thoughts, you miss your opportunity to help.

Useless thoughts are an obstacle to growth.

Thought Control

Thought creates.

Mind is matter to build with — you will understand this when you begin to see on higher planes.

You must not let your mind run free as a little dog but control it constantly and take its leadership into your own hands.

Control of thought is the most important step in all things.

Never be negative where it concerns your thoughts: keep watch constantly.

Every one of your thoughts must reach Me so that I can link them to Mine.

And My thoughts must be received by your brain always more distinctly.

Train and train that thought body.

Train it by thinking clearly — and thinking only of what will help others.

Purify it, and quiet it. Try to shut off thoughts that have nothing to do with the subject at hand.

Make it more sensitive and pure — then, We can use it always.

Pure thoughts are materials for Us to work with.

Purify your thoughts to such a degree that every one of them can be used by Us and by Him.

Purify them by measuring them with His.

Use your brain as thinking capacity to its utmost power, and many obscure points will become clear and understood.

Your ego can be reached by concentrated thinking.

Be concentrated on whatever you do, hear, study, or read. The power of thought is great. Use it consciously, now, for Him. Always use it to help the world.

Every day is lost on which you have not trained the mind and put it in better shape to be used for Us and Him.

Silence

Your acts must prove your stage — not your words.

Learn to be silent.

Speak little, and help others.

These are the things for a pupil of the Master to learn.

You cannot be Our instrument so long as the lesson of silence is not fully understood and applied.

It is much wiser to be silent than to speak where talk is unnecessary.

Only use your lips to help others — no more for your own interests and pleasures.

Your discipline is to watch every word; yes, every word.

Learn to listen when others speak — and, in the meantime, help the speaker by mental force.

Never wish to shine, nor to speak to anyone about yourself, unless you are quite sure that by so doing, you help that person — and that is very rarely the case.

Never gossip about others, not even in an innocent way.

Talk about others only when you can help or defend them in their absence.

Do not say of anyone what you would not want them to hear.

If you subdue the words before they pass over your lips, you help yourself; you help others — and by doing so, work for Us because We are the others.

You must also be active as a silent worker for the forces of the Light.

Be still, and yet active: still for the outer world, and active to reach Me.

Try hard and constantly — and you will soon be able to control speech and thought.

Truth

All that unites is truth. All that separates is falsehood.

It is not enough that a thing is true: if it is worthwhile to repeat it, it must also be helpful.

A thing may be true and kind, but if it is not helpful to mention it to somebody, it is a waste of force to do so.

Never say something that is not absolutely true.

Be truthful in speech and in thought.

Be accurate in all you do — true and precise in all your acts, words, and thoughts.

If you are not, you can never be entrusted with important work.

Every hour, think of the Truth of which He is the living symbol.

Let the Truth shine through you.

Live that which is in you, that which you are. All else is false.

Purity

Purer than the snow must your feelings be.

Become pure — pure like everything that is purer than you are now.

Will to be pure. We shall help you then.

You will succeed if you have faith — faith in Our strength and in Our wish to help you.

Your first duty to yourself and the world is to purify your thoughts.

They must be worthy of passing through Him and carrying His force.

The more you can impress the higher, purer thoughts upon your brain, the easier it will be for you to live them — because that should be the result.

Make pure the instruments: through a soiled instrument, My light can never shine.

The purer the instruments, the better tools they are for Us to use.

Purify the three bodies — and feel the power to express love grow within you.

Become pure glass, through which His light can reach and illuminate the world.

Become pure as the living light, which streams out of His Heart, His Being.

Incessantly keep yourself within the rays of His purifying Light and Glory.

Live in His world of purity and light.

Health

Build up strong instruments for My use so that they may not be shattered to pieces by My force when I want to use them for the great work.

We are helping you to improve them as much as karma permits.

But you have to restore what was once spoiled: you must undo the results of past shortcomings and ignorance.

A strong body that can stand the strain of training and work is what We want if you wish to serve Us and pour out Our forces for the helping of the world.

Use your common sense, telling you your instrument must be in tune before you can do things for Us.

You have to look after it with love for Us — and for it, too, for We want it to be strong.

Strengthen it — make it pure and reliable.

All will depend on your own efforts.

Work with physical and spiritual laws — try to live according to both.

The one reflects on the other, as both are manifestations of one and the same thing.

Study the Law — and follow its effects in physical matter.

Law must be maintained on all planes.

Overworking is a spiritual as much as a physical failure — and the reaction always proves this.

Too little action brings sickness in the end — too much action brings trouble as well.

Even the Masters rest their bodies and obey the law of physical matter.

Do not reject pure joy and recreation.

Take time to relax in nature: sunshine and air are just as necessary as relaxation.

Overcome the weakness of the body by poise and equilibrium.

Surround yourself with rhythmic vibrations — and give them to others.

Think rightly, and you can bring about better physical conditions.

Think beauty and better health will be the result.

Think strength and strength will come to you.

Will your body to be strong, and work to make it strong.

Will to be strong to help others — and soon, health will come.

Strength

Grow in inner strength — then will the outer be yours when you need it for My work.

The strength of the whole Universe is there to help you.

There is a strength that can always be felt and always be lived: that of your own divinity.

Express that more and more, and your body will soon obey its master.

Never expect to use the amount of strength you have in two different ways.

Use it only for His work and all that makes His Path easier.

Learn to preserve energy; learn to use your forces to the best advantage for others — not for yourself.

Save strength in the less important things so that you have some when you need it.

Become a force in yourself, and do not depend so much on outer circumstances.

Come to Me by your strength; throw off all that is in your way.

Strive ever harder to accomplish what will bring My power to you.

Have Me in your thoughts always, and draw My strength toward you.

Learn to use My force instead of your own.

You can help that way much better than when you use up all your own energy.

Use your strength wisely — and more will be given to you.

Rule Your Bodies

Watch your vehicles. Learn to master them.

Train them to obey your will.

Use your power to control the forces which are playing through them.

Learn to separate yourself from the lower bodies, and — without losing the controlling power — use them as your tools.

Every day, take time to do this and see them as existing only for your use.

Try to live life outside your bodies — and train them consciously to obey the real "*you*."

Stand aside serenely and with determination to let Me work through them.

In a strong physical body, you can better control the other vehicles.

The physical one alone cannot make you ready for better work. The others also want to be so strong that even in sleep, no influence can overtake them.

The astral body must remain unruffled and quiet.

Still your mental body, too — do it often: it needs that.

Never confuse the longings of the astral and mental bodies with your inner Voice.

Make a definite effort to distinguish between intuition and impulse.

If you keep your lower vehicles under constant control, you will have no difficulty knowing which is which.

Never again listen to unworthy impulses.

Cheerfulness

Cheerfulness is your best healer; live in joy and strength.

Serene cheerfulness is a quality that helps even in sorrow.

New strength will be poured into you when you learn how to respond to the light and bright side of life, which must be expressed by Our disciples.

Be strong and cheerful on your path upward — and do not let unimportant things have the power to weaken your perseverance to attain.

Be hopeful and strong.

Life must flow through you in all its brightness and strength.

Be of good cheer always — and look into the past with no sorrow or feeling that you should have done better.

Failure is only in ceasing to strive. All the rest is growth — even where you do not see it.

Be cheerful and have no care — because We are with you.

Happiness

Always think of the happiness of others, and add to it wherever you can.

This is what you must work for — asking nothing for yourself, giving all you have to diminish the suffering and need of others.

Happiness exists in freely giving all that is yours to others.

Focus your consciousness on diminishing the world's cruelty and ignorance — helping the powers which work for the joy and happiness of erring humanity.

Become a beam of light, and make the world happier with your presence.

You so work for Us.

Think happy thoughts: there is enough sadness in the world.

Change the vibrations of sadness by opposite ones.

Nature can help you to do that better than anything else.

Go to her, who is your real Mother; drink in her breath, and be one with her flowers and sunshine.

Go among the hills and mountains, and respond to their strength and joyous serenity.

Let your life and theirs become one in the great oneness of all — and be thrilled with their happiness and beauty.

Life is worth living if you can only rise above your self-made limitations.

Love others — and in that love, feel happy.

Joy

Dare to live, will to give — become life, and vibrate joy.

Make your life one ray of joy for others!

Be happy and strong — and feel gratitude for being able to work for Him, the Lord of all Glory, all Joy!

Become light-bringers, giving His message of joy and liberty to all.

To work for Him must be joy and happiness, and never may be felt as a sad duty.

Feel joyful and strong — and think of beautiful things and work you can do.

Increase the love and beauty in the world; make others feel the beauty of love and kindness.

Life is joy and strength, power and fullness — and humanity must learn to express it in all its glorious greatness and beauty.

Love supreme must reign, and purity and exalted joy await their expression through humankind.

Vibrate joy: the joy of helping others.

Spread joy and good feelings around you, and affect everybody so they feel better and stronger for meeting you.

Our disciples must become like living sunshine and light to all they contact.

The real joy of existence is in giving.

Learn that joy — and respond to the all-embracing love of the Divine, which is joy and power.

Laugh with the sky — sing with the birds — breathe with the flowers — and love with God's love.

Worry Not

Do not increase the suffering of the world by worrying.

Always think of others, and by doing so, forget the little self with its petty worries.

Only selfish disappointments and longings bring feelings of depression. They belong to the personality which still wants things for itself.

Overcome the power of influences and surroundings: they belong to the past and must not have the power to tie you down.

Think of Us, your Elders: how much We have to carry on Our shoulders — but We never worry.

Think of your Master, who is happy and strong — and of whom you are a part.

Remember that in Our World, depression and discontent are unknown.

Go out in nature.

Look to the trees, flowers, and birds, and be one with them.

They worry not but love life — and you must do the same.

You must not worry about anything, for whatever happens to you is with Our purpose.

Do you not know that what I do is well done — and that you could not change the working of the Law as it is destined that things shall be?

I am always near, and My strength can be used by you if you do not shut yourself off by depression or nervousness.

Do not feel discouraged in your efforts to understand the Law.

Do the best you can — and leave the rest to Us.

You may not worry, and you may not feel depressed — because then, even We cannot help you.

Will

There is only one Will — and you must now learn to reach that Higher Will, the Self of All.

Will is the foundation upon which the Universe rests.

Develop that power — and know that you are will, as well as wisdom.

There is nothing that the God within you cannot achieve.

Nothing is impossible when will is directed with one-pointedness and understanding.

Will is all-powerful.

It is in you — bring it out.

Make one great effort — and old thought forms, old habits, will fall away as darkness before the sun.

Break the shell of former causes, and become the maker of all things.

You must succeed if you know your own power.

Your will and determination to choose the good and pure are enough to call Us down to you.

In your will is your destiny.

Be self-willed — and yet sensitive.

Every second, I must be in your consciousness and fill both heart and mind.

By linking your consciousness to Mine, you do not lose your individual will — because your true Will is I.

Your true Will understands. It is wisdom.

Try and try and try — and will and will and will!

And you will be helped by Us — but you must dare and will.

Work!

Work, and show your love in work.

Work! There is only one word: work — work for Him.

Make your work an offering to Him.

Do His work with joy and gratitude in your heart.

Work hard: in thought, in speech, and act — and so, influence your surroundings and create purer conditions around you.

You must work, work, work incessantly for others, for humanity.

Unselfish work must be your only thought.

The one thought of work must be so strong that it pushes aside little hurts and wrongs. They do not matter and are the means of bringing out your growing strength.

Try to work with all — and as one with all.

Watch small opportunities, and you will be ready for the greater ones when you are called to fulfill greater and always greater responsibilities.

There is much little work to be learned and done before the greater can come.

Every day, you have opportunities to help others to carry their burdens and make their lives easier and happier.

Do as much as possible — and as much as seems wise.

Work and work, whenever you think you can do it — and rest sufficiently to do more work afterward.

When Our work requires it, then there is Our strength to do it.

Live for the work which you can do for Us.

Work steadily and persistently to become one with Our love — then all can be helped through you by Us.

No effort must be too great to give others of Our love.

Act Our love for all. Pass it on to all beings.

Make love the motive for all your words, all your deeds.

Work — work incessantly, in some way.

Thousands of ways there are to help Him.

Every minute can be used.

Every day, you will find work to do that you did not think of before.

Use discrimination in all you do — and you will soon eliminate things that waste your energy.

We never tell Our workers what work is most needed. They must look around the world and do what circumstances require.

Work — an uncountable amount of work — is waiting to be done by the ones who will make themselves fit to do it.

Our work is a glorious one, the outcome of which reaches far beyond your conception.

The world is in a crisis — and in preparation for the Coming, much hard work must be done.

Every disciple is used to the utmost of their strength, and every effort is intensified.

Do not miss your opportunities. We can only help those who can be used for Our work.

The all-important thing is humble service — giving all, asking nothing. Working, no matter if blame or praise, is the outcome.

The time is short.

It is now that We can use every effort for good.

Now is the time to work for Him!

Go wherever you can to do His work.

Try to make the world realize His nearness.

Go on — and do things which will help His Coming.

III

EVER
ONWARD!

Leave your petty world of frivolous fancies, and enter into your real possession of power and greatness.

Live the Life

You know what is required: bring into practice what We have taught.

Always do the very highest that you can do.

Never forget that you reap the karma of all you do — and when you lack in any of the teachings given to you, you must reap the consequences.

All your efforts must be to help evolution and become an expression of light and love.

No effort will fail, which is made to forward evolution toward the Light of Truth.

Be willing to serve Us — and in serving, you will come ever nearer to Our wisdom, Our love.

Strive to understand the Law. Work and live in harmony with it, and use it for your growth.

Learn the power of life — learn the beauty of love.

Obey your heart, and count not the consequences.

Think of head, heart, and hand as the Trinity in yourself — and you will never make a mistake if you let them work as one.

Do not spend your time in trifles anymore.

Do not waste any force to strengthen things that you know stand between you and the fuller expression of your true Self.

Forget small things, and you can grasp the greater truths.

Create an entirely new way of thinking and acting — and only do worthwhile things to be done by Our disciples.

Live Our Law: Love — and the rest will come in time.

Reaching Up

Few are Our disciples, and they have many tasks.

You, who have the longing to help the world: do not hesitate to use the means to help you reach your purpose.

Reach up to Us — and nothing is impossible.

Reach up to Us — by reaching out to others in love and compassion.

Your whole being must become the link between others and the Light. Every word must express Our love and help to all who can receive it.

Strive every day to reach Us and to live in Our World.

Never think that the inner work is less important than the outer: you must be before you can give.

Seek to obtain, so you may give.

Wish, even long, for spiritual possession — with the desire to help others with it.

Then, shall all be given unto you.

Help always — and trust the God within.

Be strong and determined in your effort, and you will increasingly realize your oneness with Us.

You must be one with Us and Our work in the world of pain and confusion.

See the instability of physical objects around you — and know them as only temporarily real.

The unreal may no longer have so much power over you.

Rise above it — and live in the eternal.

First, raise your consciousness to where you can listen and hear Our Voice.

Do that when you are concentrating on your work, and always do that in your touch with others.

Do it more and more — until you do it always.

Yes: raise your consciousness to Us — and We come down to you. We come down to your world when it can help.

You may call on Us always for help and strength.

Burn away the dross, which still separates you from the Divine Light, with the purity of unselfish efforts.

Seek the Light evermore. It is there, and you are part of it.

Develop your inner strength — and live in the higher part of your being.

Give your whole life now to Us.

Be a Channel

Open up yourself for Our power — only then can We work through you.

Your work is to purify and widen the channel by which We — your true Self — can work in the world of shadows.

Make that channel ever purer, stronger, and better in every way for Our expression.

Kill out all desire for self. Ask nothing for yourself — and you will soon be Our dear vehicle through which Our light can shine into the world.

Let the little personality always get smaller — and give Us more power of expression in its instruments.

Then can We ever express more of Ourselves in them — and give to all Our instruments, as We can reach them through yours.

The more you open up for Us, you will be helped to see, understand, and realize that We are you and that you are We.

You are We, and We are you — just as much as you allow Our force to play through you upon others.

Seek Us — become Us — live Our life!

Meditate on oneness with Us. The more you do that, the better We can work through you — and by so doing, help you, too.

Spare no effort to reach your goal.

Untiring efforts will bring the wished-for results.

Waver not, and be strong.

Master and Pupil

Think of Me as your Master helping you — and yet, of Me as your Higher Self, which is yourself.

Make yourself always more and more One with Me.

You must become I, as I am He.

In the highest aspect, you and I are One.

Keep your mind fixed on Me.

Open yourself more for My force — and look upon yourself as the instrument I use.

Feel Me within you.

Try to express Me to the world I love.

Always think of yourself as if in My presence — and feel My touch in all you do and think.

Obey My slightest warning. Learn to hear Me, even in the greatest confusion of physical life.

Listen, and only think of Me as speaking to you in your heart.

I am always there.

When a pupil is accepted, a channel is made through which a Master can communicate with them.

The pupil's task is to open up that channel more and more and make it wider through their efforts — so that more of their Master can reach them.

Do not allow that link to get clogged from your side by old thoughts and habits which cannot pass to Me.

Constantly draw on My force. By doing so, the channel will become ever wider — and more of Me can come to you.

Always be open to My powers — of which so much can reach you, as you can use in your vehicles.

Never forget that you are Our vehicle in the world of humankind.

Be firmly determined to become an expression of love and helpfulness everywhere where you can give.

Our love for Our disciples is greater than you can know.

Radiate that love in your world — and We will always send you more to use.

Be a key that others can use to enter that kingdom of unselfish purity and love, which is Our World.

All that can help others to see the beauty and purity of Our World must be manifested by you.

Stand on your own feet.

A disciple must be able to stand alone — alone with their Master.

Many years may pass in which you will not see or hear Me nor feel My presence, but I am there just the same.

We are with Our disciples in all their trials and tests — and We will never fail you.

I am always there when you really seek Me — whether you feel My presence or not.

Nothing, from now on, may come between you and Us.

You cannot separate yourself from Us if you follow the Voice of Love and unselfishness.

I know that all this training is hard — but use your will, and you can grow very fast.

Throw away your fear of insidious powers.

See the Light — and be the Light. They and the Light can never manifest together.

Live Our life. Think Our thoughts. Do Our work.

Become a living example of Our qualities — and so, make the world happier, purer, and better.

My love protects you.

The Path

Grow in love and self-sacrifice. Live for others; make yourself useful to others — that is the Path.

The Path is the Path of the Cross — and its burden will be felt by all who want to become like Him.

You will have to suffer for every step which brings you nearer to Him.

Think of all who have trodden the same Path before you and all who will come after you — and you will never hesitate.

Go on bravely, and let Our love be enough for you to fight the battle.

You will never feel its pain when you have your consciousness turned to Us.

The Path is joy and strength. With every step you take, you will feel its power.

The joy of eternal consciousness awaits the weary pilgrim at the end of each victory over the power of matter.

Be strong — and never despair.

The Way to the Great Brotherhood

You have all the possibilities of Divinity within you. You now must bring them into reality and manifest the qualities which will bring you there.

Develop your inherent powers.

Express all that is waiting for expression.

Dare, dare, dare!

We need helpers who dare to face things and do things for Us.

Know yourself as We know you — and then improve yourself to what We want you to be.

Look upon all other human beings as expressions of Divine Life; they will all be some time what We are now.

This must be your definite purpose now: to become what We are.

We are waiting for you to be ready.

The world is waiting to see Our work done.

Every day, good work must be done for Us.

Think of Our purpose, Our aim to help humanity — and then, you will always know what to do.

You can never fail when you work with Our tools.

Endeavor harder and harder to be worthy of being used by Us.

Nothing is ever done in vain that is done with this motive behind it: to bring others nearer to happiness and to understanding.

Life must be used in all its potency.

Life, ever-glorious life, is your expression — and soon, you will feel its power vibrate through you.

Your way is clear.

Go ahead with all your strength and use your energy to climb steadily and constantly.

Approach that realization of Oneness, which you must feel before initiation occurs.

Once the Gate swings open — and once the Light is seen — all will be easier.

Work with all your strength to shorten the way which separates you from that moment when you will speak the word for which all have to stand aside.

Give full force to all that has to be mastered before We can open Our door for you — before you can enter the Great Brotherhood as a member of Our ranks.

You have knocked. Now work, and We will receive you when you work hard enough.

Initiation is the crowning touch of personal efforts.

Double your efforts!

Make up your mind to attain, and you will.

You know now what is expected of you — now, do it!

Children of the Light

Fulfill your mission, O children of the Light!

Do not hesitate to break your fetters of the past. Tread the path to power and reality by shaking off your iron chains of unworthy selfishness.

Lift your faces to the light of love and everlasting beauty, and follow Him, your Guide and God, toward redemption and freedom.

Realize your true inner being, and obey the Voice of heavenly Mercy, which can be heard by all — and soon will be among you.

O people of Divine destiny — open your hearts for His love. Melt the crust of ignorant selfishness around your hearts, and give freedom to your imprisoned God by obeying the longing for love which beats in every breast and pulsates in every atom.

Receive Him — prepare yourself for His light-giving nearness, and be worthy of your rights and privileges.

Sing His praise in all you do; build His love in all you contact; live His Law of Understanding and Oneness — and so, you will become that for which you came into manifested existence.

Childhood is over.

Face the difficulties of attainment — and fight for your freedom with Christ-like strength and all-conquering perseverance.

Look around you — and see Him in all.

Listen, and you can catch His call to you:

UNFOLD AND BECOME WHAT YOU ARE

THANK YOU FOR READING!

IF YOU ENJOYED THIS BOOK, please consider leaving a review, even if it is only a line or two. It would make all the difference and would be very much appreciated.

Sign up for our newsletter to be the first to know when new books are published:

radiantbooks.co/bonus

Made in the USA
Las Vegas, NV
10 October 2023

78803750R00060